How Shall They Hear?

Memoirs and observations of a country preacher

John Mollitt

Onwards and Upwards Publishers

3 Radfords Turf
Cranbrook
EX5 7DX
United Kingdom

www.onwardsandupwards.org

Published in the UK by Onwards and Upwards Publishers (2016).

ISBN: 978-1-911086-43-7
Typeface: Sabon LT
Graphic design: LM Graphic Design

About the Author

John Mollitt was born in the Lune Valley, near to Lancaster. Having worked in banking and the Civil Service, he became Pastor of Ingleton Evangelical Church, North Yorkshire in 1979. He retired in 2009 and is now engaged in an itinerant preaching ministry.

John is married to Pat and has three children and five grandchildren. He enjoys watching sport, playing chess and has a nostalgic interest in steam railways.

Endorsements

John and Pat have been involved in rural ministry for over forty years, and John's reminiscing is both heart-warming and at times amusing. Preaching his first sermon to his brother at the age of ten, he later proclaimed the gospel widely in the open air, at children's missions, throughout a long-serving pastorate and now in an itinerant ministry to rural fellowships. This has provided John not only with a score of anecdotes, but more significantly with a sympathetic understanding of the life of small village churches.

Simply told, John's humble reflections on his own ministry and the sad decline of our nation's spiritual health will be of interest to all who know him and who have been aware of John and Pat's loving and selfless care for their adopted son Aaron who, with multiple physical and mental disabilities, died in 2016 at the age of twenty-eight.

I warmly commend *How Shall They Hear?* to the many who have enjoyed John's ministry when on holiday at Ingleton and to a wider readership.

Brian H. Edwards
Christian Author
www.brianedwards.org.uk

Not every book I edit is a joy to read but from the first page of *How Shall They Hear?* I knew it was going to be a pleasure. John's down-to-earth memoirs of his life as a preacher are honest and humorous and I heartily recommend them to any reader.

Andrew Halloway
Editor, Good News newspaper;
Freelance Editor

Contents

Foreword by Mark Thomas

I smiled with much recognition as I read through the first pages of John's book where he describes settings, communities and churches familiar to my own roots and travels around this neck of the woods and county boundaries. It also brought back memories of personalities and characters known to us both.

In particular, stirred up are recollections of the Warehouse days in Carnforth with Stuart and Jill Briscoe, and of a special night when Dr John Hunter shared Christ and "sceptic" John (as he called himself) responded to God's grace and began a new life. From locally known John Pratt to nationally recognized pastor and writer Dr Martyn Lloyd-Jones, this book shows the important impact that other believers can have upon our early Christian lives and in preparing a young preacher to be a means of sharing the same message that everyone needs to hear.

These are genuine and humorous "memoirs and observations of a county preacher" and for any of the same vintage as John and I, this record of his experiences will take any churchgoer who knows the circuit down memory lane, enabling recollection of what the 'good old days' in church were like. Hard pews, Sunday School outings, sleepy farmers and "Jesus wants me for a sunbeam" will create their own pictures in the mind as the book is read.

For some, then, these pages will arouse a legitimate sense of nostalgia and thankfulness, while others will be challenged by the commitment of the writer through his pastoral life to share Christ with others and the need to be ready to do so whether in the pulpit, on the street, at home, with the known or the unknown; for as the title exclaims, "How shall they hear?" This book will prompt the reader to recognise that in every generation – for the teenagers, gamblers, respectable church attendees – the gospel of Christ "is the power of God to salvation for everyone who believes" (Romans 1:16, NKJV).

Throughout there are fascinating and funny tales of the preacher's lot woven into the importance of establishing a true biblical basis for proclaiming the gospel of Christ and the joy of seeing the fruit of God's Spirit at work bringing salvation to those who hear, whether in the open air or under a roof.

God's history has proved that He will not fail to have the message of Christ promulgated throughout all time and the reader is encouraged to see those who have gone before as unashamed of the gospel and encouragers to others to take up the baton. This, of course, is the content of Hebrews 13:7. "Remember your leaders, who spoke the word of God to you. Consider the outcome of their way of life and imitate their faith." (NIV)

In Pat, John's wife, he has had both vital companion and co-worker in the midst of church responsibilities and challenges, which should be a great example to any budding preacher or pastor with the sharing of the load as well as the gospel. Aaron could not be missed out, as he became such an integral and important part of family life, church life and a wonderful illustration of love and life restored, as well as a gospel message in himself.

Called to preach or not, this read is certainly a heart-warming personal account of a country preacher's life but with the overriding intention to encourage and challenge 'pulpit and pew' to proclaim the Lord Jesus Christ for all to hear. True life now and forever is found in Him alone.

Mark Thomas
Capernwray Missionary Fellowship

How then shall they call on Him
in whom they have not believed?
And how shall they believe in Him
of whom they have not heard?
And how shall they hear
without a preacher?
And how shall they preach
unless they are sent?
As it is written:
'How beautiful are the feet of those who
preach the gospel of peace,
who bring glad tidings of good things!' …
So then faith comes by hearing,
and hearing by the word of God.

Romans 10:14-15,17 (NKJV)

CHAPTER ONE

Childhood Memories

MY FIRST SERMON WAS PREACHED at the tender age of nine or ten. Not, you understand, in a city church or a village chapel but in the front room of our home in Ruskin Drive, Morecambe.

One week I was the preacher and the next week my twin brother, Jim, was the preacher. We always had a better service when I was the preacher, not because I was a better speaker but because Jim was able to tap out a hymn tune on the piano with one finger. His repertoire was somewhat limited and I recall 'God Save Our Gracious Queen' being sung with some regularity!

To Twenty-First Century ears, it may seem a strange way for boys to spend a Sunday morning, but perhaps not too strange in the 1950s when, for quite a number of families, Sunday was still centred on the church. There was never any doubt that we would be at the 10.30am and 6.30pm services, as well as Sunday School at 2pm.

Sunday services were not 'child friendly' and we were expected to be 'seen but not heard'. However, the first minister I remember at Bare Methodist Church in Morecambe – Rev. Arthur Marshall – did have a 'little black bag' and he would talk to the children about an object produced from the bag. This was the same Arthur Marshall who, when at a meeting and the chairman said, "Rev. Marshall will now give his address," stood up and announced, "67 Broadway, Morecambe," and then walked out! He was apparently annoyed that the chairman had given him so little time in which to speak.

The only concession to our age group was a wine gum or a midget gem at different points in the sermon. That is not to say there were no lighter moments. When the sermon started, the organist Mr R. got up from the organ stool and sat next to his wife in the choir. Within minutes, he was in the 'land of nod' and remained so until, as the sermon concluded, he was vigorously nudged in the ribs by Mrs R. I am not sure he could have sung, "I was bruised but Jesus healed me," but I expect he could have sung, "I was bruised!"

Another 'sleeper' was Fred – a chimney sweep and property repairer by day, which also included the Lord's Day. He worshipped every Sunday night but usually arrived just before the start of the sermon. Perhaps even sooner than Mr R., Fred was asleep and he too was dependent on the good offices of his wife to get him awake and ready for the last hymn. On a church anniversary weekend, Fred related how as a baby he had been brought to the church by his mother and had slept throughout the services. A man was heard to quip, "Nothing has changed, Fred – you still do!"

On another occasion, I can remember being in the evening service at Tewitfield Methodist Church, near Carnforth, when we were plunged into darkness by an electricity failure. Torches came out and were pointed at the preacher, enabling him to continue his sermon. Some fifty-five years later, I was privileged to preach at the Tewitfield Methodist Church Anniversary services.

An elderly preacher, much to our amusement, constantly referred to Paul and Barnstaple in his sermon. The same preacher, on telling a friend he had "been in Bedford a week" was asked, "Oh, have you not been very well?" Another elderly preacher – were they really old or did they just seem to be old to me? – much to our amusement, accidentally turned over two pages in his bible and continued reading. He had the air of a man who knew that something was not quite right but he made no comment.

I may not have understood much of the services but I never remember being bored. School was not as interactive as it is today, so having to sit quietly for an hour was not difficult.

Bare was a retirement area of Morecambe and so, not surprisingly, the congregation was somewhat elderly. Most of the ladies wore hats, and when I asked my mother the name of one lady who was wearing an enormous hat, I was told she was called Mrs Hatton! Though it is sixty years ago, I can still remember the names of many in that congregation and how kind and encouraging they were to me and my brother.

The church was regularly full on a Sunday morning but, perhaps due to the age of the congregation, only a handful attended the 6.30pm service. As a child, I was puzzled as to why many of those who were 'too old' to get to church at 6.30pm on a Sunday were never too old for a pie and pea supper at 7.30pm on a Saturday!

In the 1950s churches, like most houses of the time, had not been built for comfort. The pews were hard, but they only ever caused a problem when they had been newly varnished. I can remember some summer Sundays when my shirt was stuck to the back of the pew and, jerking forward, I fully expected my bare back to be exposed to the congregation.

As a seven-year-old, I attended a service the significance of which I was only to discover many years later. It was in August 1955 and we were on holiday in London. Whether the holiday had been planned to coincide with the event I am not sure, but we were at the farewell service for the late Rev. W. E. Sangster, who was leaving Westminster Central Hall in London after sixteen years of ministry. Every Sunday evening he had a congregation of three thousand; some people queued for an hour to get into the service.

His text for his final service was from Acts 20:31-32 (KJV): "Therefore watch, and remember, that by the space of three years I ceased not to warn every one night and day with tears. And now, brethren, I commend you to God, and to the word of his grace, which is able to build you up, and to give you an inheritance among all them which are sanctified." I know this not because I remember the sermon but because I read it in Paul Sangster's biography of his father! Dr Sangster was a renowned evangelical Methodist, and years later I was to profit from his books and writings.

Sunday school was more age-appropriate and songs such as 'Jesus wants me for a sunbeam' and 'Hear the pennies dropping' were sung with gusto. It was all in the days before any interaction, and we sat round in a half circle, motionless, as the teacher told the Bible story. Mr Wilson, our teacher, was very patient – and he needed to be, as some weeks he got up from his chair with a sticky lollipop wrapper attached to his trousers!

Summer brought with it two annual events. The first was the crowning of the Sunday School queen. This was held in the grounds of a private school; the school being owned by our Sunday School Superintendent, Miss Laity. As six-year-olds, Jim and I were chosen to be page boys at the ceremony. At the time, this 'honour' perhaps filled me with pride, but on seeing photographs many years later, it just filled me with embarrassment.

The second summer 'ritual' was the Sunday School trip to a farm at Ings – just a few miles from Windermere. I went for several years and the sun always seemed to be shining. In the austere 1950s, before the advent of overseas package holidays, Sunday School trips had a special appeal and the coach was always crowded.

Christmas also had two regular events. The Sunday School nativity was held on the Sunday before Christmas, and though I wished to be Joseph or a wise man, it never happened. Instead, hiding under the pews in the choir stalls, I would emerge either dressed in white sheets as part of the angelic choir or with a towel around my head as a shepherd. The other event was the Christmas party, which always included a visit from Father Christmas and ended with the singing of 'Auld Lang Syne'.

Another reason for having our own Sunday service may have been that there were preachers in the family. My grandfather, born in 1880, began preaching for the Methodist Church in 1898, and was presented with a seventy-year preaching certificate just before he died in hospital in 1968. And on the wall of my study I have the framed certificate which he received in 1948, on completing fifty years as a Local Preacher. His preaching was not confined to the Methodist Church, and I have a Bible commentary presented to him to recognise fifty years of preaching at Caton Baptist Church.

I only ever heard Grandfather preach once. He was staying with us in Morecambe for ten days, and I travelled with him on the bus as he went to take the morning service at the Independent Methodist Church in Lancaster. I cannot recall the sermon he preached but his talk to the children was based on the feeding of the five thousand.

Recently, when I was taking a mid-week meeting at Wray Methodist Church, I met a man who could vividly recall a sermon preached by my grandfather well over fifty years earlier. His text had been Hebrews 2:9 (KJV): "We see Jesus ... crowned with glory and honour." He had finished with the challenge, "Is Jesus crowned – is he on the throne of your heart?"

Grandfather is also remembered for his Christian character. A lady commented on the impression he had made upon her when she was a young girl: "Your grandfather was such a lovely man that whenever he came to the Mission, I thought it was Jesus in the pulpit."

My grandfather had been a signalman on the railways and he not only prepared sermons in the signal box but on occasions, in the box, he would hold a prayer meeting with one of the porters. This was, of course, long before the days of political correctness or Health and Safety initiatives.

His funeral service was held on a wintry Saturday afternoon in December 1968, but such were the numbers attending that the police had to direct the traffic from the Methodist church at Brookhouse to the churchyard at Quernmore.

With my father having died when I was just eight years of age, 'Granddad' was a well-loved and important figure in my life. He died some six months before I was converted, but I have no doubt that his life and prayers were instrumental in my coming to faith and, later, in my own call to preach.

I also had an uncle, John Pratt, who was a well-known preacher. He had his own poultry business but lectured at Capernwray Hall in England and in

Germany. He was appointed Minister of Capernwray Evangelical Church in 1976 and pastored the church until his sudden death in 1980. I preached with him at camp meetings in the area, and one Monday night I deputised for him at Lowgill Methodist Church. It was a Harvest Thanksgiving service and Uncle was double-booked.

I sometimes feel that his 'mantle' has fallen on me as over the years and increasingly in retirement I have taken services, Bible studies and funerals at Capernwray Evangelical Church. The church is only a twenty-minute ride from Ingleton, and many of the older members still speak of my uncle with affection.

CHAPTER TWO

Early Years of Preaching

AS THE 1950s TURNED INTO the 1960s and I went from being a child to a teenager, any thoughts of preaching were soon extinguished. An evangelical upbringing was not able to withstand liberal preaching and the influence of R.E. teachers, who all but destroyed my faith in the Scriptures.

The teenage years are impressionable, and when well-educated men questioned or denied fundamental doctrines, I all too readily imbibed what they were saying. Added to which, some of these men were not just ministers and teachers, they were also friends. One of these ministers took Jim and me to our first professional football match; a memorable game, in which Burnley beat Manchester United by six goals to one at Turf Moor, on Boxing Day, 1963. Friends and 'experts' in religion – who was I to question what they said?

This was all to change in 1969 when I was invited to a Sunday night young people's meeting being held at the Warehouse in Carnforth. The preacher that June evening was Dr John Hunter from Capernwray Hall, and through the grace of God I was converted and the sceptic became a Christian.

The Warehouse was an outreach work led by Stuart and Jill Briscoe from Capernwray Hall. Jill had been challenged and inspired by reading Malachi 3:10 (NKJV): "'Bring all the tithes into the storehouse, that there may be food in My house, and try Me now in this,' says the Lord of hosts, 'if I will not open for you the windows of heaven and pour out for you such blessing that there will not be room enough to receive it.'" This was truly of the Lord. Many young people first heard the gospel and came to personal faith in Christ at the Warehouse.

Capernwray Hall had become the property of the Thomas family in 1946, and since 1947 has been in continuous use as a Christian centre. Dr Hunter trained as a teacher before working as an evangelist with Capernwray Missionary Fellowship of Torchbearers. I met him again at a ministers' fraternal at Capernwray Hall in 1984 and was able to share with him how he had been instrumental in my conversion. Dr Hunter went to be with the Lord in October 2005 at the age of ninety-six.

"If any man be in Christ, he is a new creature," (2 Corinthians 5:17, KJV) and my 'newness' showed itself in a changed attitude to the Bible. From being a book I felt free to criticise and to dismantle, it now became a book I respected and revered. It was the

Word of God. Of course, the book had not changed but I had, and I saw it in an entirely new light.

Within weeks of my conversion I felt an inward compulsion to 'preach the Word', and without that inner work of the Spirit I would never have contemplated such a calling. Whilst the inner call has to be confirmed by the church, it is, I believe, the necessary prerequisite before any preaching is undertaken. In the words of the Apostle Paul, "Woe is unto me, if I preach not the gospel!" (1 Corinthians 9:16, KJV)

I was accepted 'on note' by the Methodist Church, which had an excellent way of training preachers. You started 'on note', which meant you went with an experienced preacher and began by announcing the hymns and doing the Bible readings. In the providence of God, I was assigned to a godly man – a Mr Bond, who taught me the privilege but also the awesome responsibility that rested upon a preacher.

From being 'on note' one progressed to being 'on trial'. This meant you were now able to take the entire service, and my first appointment was at Bare Methodist Church in Morecambe. As this was my own local church it was a daunting occasion, but the congregation was most supportive and sought to encourage a faltering, nervous preacher.

One had to take a Local Preachers' exam and preach a trial sermon before being fully accredited as a lay preacher. I preached my trial sermon at Torrisholme Methodist Church and became a fully fledged preacher at a Recognition Service in December 1969. I still have the bible presented to me on that occasion, signed by Rev. Brian S. O'Gorman, who was President of the Methodist Conference that year.

It was through preaching that I was to meet my future wife. Pat was a member of Heysham Methodist Church and in August 1970 I was invited to speak at their Christian Endeavour meeting. Christian Endeavour was begun in the USA in 1881 by a young Congregational minister, Dr Francis Clark. He wanted an organisation which would help Christians to grow in their faith and be trained for the Lord's service. The movement catered for all ages but its main emphasis was on young people. Christian Endeavour grew rapidly and continues today, although with the advent of other such meetings, it has for a number of years been in decline in the UK. My grandfather always had a C.E. badge in his lapel, and for many years he was the leader of Christian Endeavour at Brookhouse Methodist Church.

I walked Pat home from that meeting, and over forty-five years later we are still walking together. And so, if for no other reason, I have much to be grateful to Christian Endeavour for. It was a joy to be the speaker at the Christian Endeavour autumn break at Hebron Hall in Cardiff in 2013 and 2014. The party consisted mainly of elderly people, but they were a testimony to the good that Christian Endeavour had done in their lives.

The first time I preached outside of Morecambe was at Calder Vale Methodist Church, as one of the three preachers from Morecambe who were appointed to take services in the Garstang circuit. It was a Sunday evening. I did not drive and I remember crouching in the back of a van before being dropped off at the 'Chapel in the Valley'. It would be ten years before I had my own transport and so I was usually dependent on the kindness of my brothers or friends. At other times I used the bus or train and, on a few occasions, an old gearless bicycle.

In the autumn of 1972, I was booked to preach at the afternoon and evening services at Brough in Cumbria. It was their Chapel Anniversary and a friend from the Salvation Army was providing the transport and also coming to sing at the services. As we travelled on the M6, just before Tebay, there was a loud bang and the car came to a standstill. This was in the days long before mobile phones, but I used the emergency phone and managed to contact the police.

It was a 2pm service at Brough and, apparently, at 2.30pm the village policeman walked down the aisle. The congregation were understandably shocked and perhaps expecting the worst until they were informed as to what had happened.

The police took us into Tebay, where the congregation was just coming out of the Methodist church. A couple kindly invited us to their home in the village, where they gave us tea and presented us with a painting. The husband was an artist and the painting of Grasmere Church still hangs on a wall in our home. This was only the beginning of their Christian kindness, as their son later took us to the evening service at Brough before transporting us back to Morecambe.

This is surely what Jesus meant when he spoke about 'going the second mile'.

Remarkably, it was to be another forty years before another car 'malfunction' stopped me from taking a service. A puncture on the Kendal bypass meant I had to miss a morning service in Workington. I am one of the most impractical men on the planet, and therefore it is a testimony to the goodness of God that I have driven thousands of miles without mishap!

On another occasion, I was due to preach at Clapham in North Yorkshire and I decided to take the train from Morecambe. All went well until the train broke down at Wennington Station. I waited a quarter of an hour, but when the conductor could not tell me if and when the train would ever start again, I had to take action. Getting off the train and walking out of the station onto a quiet country road, I flagged down the first car that appeared. To my delight, the car stopped and the young driver, Desmond, was not only someone I knew but a Christian, on his way to see his fiancée in Ingleton. Putting his foot down, we reached Clapham just minutes before the service was due to start.

Sometimes, travelling by public transport meant not that you were late for a service but that you arrived in extra good time. When this happened, I tried to use the time profitably by giving out gospel leaflets. I recall one scorching summer afternoon doing this in Garstang town centre, and one cold December evening putting Christmas leaflets through house doors in Ingleton.

Gunnerthwaite Farm was a Sunday afternoon service I always enjoyed, and on a summer's day I chose to cycle to this appointment. Suddenly, hills appeared where I am sure they had never been before, and what I expected to be a leisurely ride turned out to be more demanding than any stage of the Tour de France. I was so exhausted and out of breath that I managed to announce the first hymn but there was no way that I could possibly sing it. I also cycled to Nether Kellet Congregational Church, where a sympathetic brother put the bicycle in the boot of his car and drove me back to Morecambe.

Ironically, the Sunday after I passed my driving test was one of the rare occasions when I had to cancel a Sunday service. I was due to preach at Ingleton on the Sunday evening, but as the snow was falling heavily in Morecambe, I knew conditions would be worse in North Yorkshire. A telephone call confirmed this was the case and a nervous, inexperienced driver was saved from making the journey.

A rather embarrassing situation was to arise some years later. I was preaching in Ripon and hospitality was being provided just a few miles from the church. I left for the evening service in reasonable time but I could not find the building. Pat has always said that I have no sense of direction, and with this being long before the days of sat navs, I was becoming ever more anxious and frustrated. Eventually, after an unwanted tour of the city, I did arrive at the church, just as a search party was about to be launched. I can still remember the time – it was two minutes after the service should have started!

On recalling this incident some years later, a preacher explained that it was always better to arrive at a service two minutes after it should have started, rather than two minutes before. His reasoning was that when you arrive with just two minutes to spare, the deacons are irritated by your lack of punctuality, whereas when you arrive two minutes after the service should have begun, the deacons are so relieved to see you that they give you a warm reception. He may be right but it's not a theory I have any inclination to test!

With most preachers having cars today, we give little thought to a previous generation of preachers who were dependent on public transport, bicycles or even a 'shanks pony'. One of my church members in Ingleton could recall a snowy January Sunday in the 1960s when a preacher walked over six miles to get to his morning appointment. I can but admire his physical fitness but also his commitment to the Lord and to His people.

My grandfather had a motorbike but never a car, and for much of his life he travelled to preaching appointments by bike. Though dressed for the elements, he must have arrived at many a service cold, wet and bedraggled. My mother could recall preachers coming on horseback – a method of transport much favoured by John Wesley!

CHAPTER THREE

Preaching in the Open Air

IN THE EARLY 1970s I BEGAN to preach in the open air, and continued until I took up the pastorate at Ingleton. A veteran of open air ministry once said to me, "If it does no one else any good, it does *me* good!" This is a sentiment I certainly agree with and I obtained many benefits through preaching in the open air. I can name four:

- it demonstrated I was not ashamed of Christ and His gospel;
- it kept me in tune with how the unconverted were thinking;
- it drove me back to God and to the Scriptures as the unconverted responded – sometimes with abuse, but at other times with serious questions;
- it was a challenge to preach in a way that was relevant and understandable.

I would emphasise that open air work in the 1970s was different to what it is today. At that time, as you preached, you could still refer to Bible characters and events as most people had some biblical knowledge. They knew who the Prodigal Son was, whereas today that is probably not the case. Another difference is that in the 1970s people would still stop at an open air meeting. I can think of summer evenings on Morecambe promenade when many would sit throughout such a service. We would offer St John's Gospels to any who wished to receive them, and most weeks there would be takers.

In summer the crowds came to us, but at other times of the year we went to the crowds. This meant visits to places such as Manchester, Liverpool and Sheffield for FA Cup ties, and from 1973-1978, on the first Saturday in May, an annual visit to Wembley Stadium for the FA Cup Final. We left Morecambe at 6am and it was 10pm before we were back. It was an exhausting but always an interesting day as we mingled with the vast crowds and sought to engage in personal conversation.

April found us at Aintree for the Grand National, where sometimes the ultra-rich showed their disdain and demonstrated that 'you cannot serve God and mammon'. However, profitable conversations were always had with some of the punters, many of whom had come across from Ireland.

Every June the Appleby Horse Fair draws hundreds of gypsies, travellers and visitors to the Cumbrian town. I remember reading Bible stories to the children in glorious sunshine and conversing with many, who listened respectfully to what we had to say. One man knew of the famous evangelist Gypsy Smith (1860-1947) and we were able to tell him that the gospel we preached was the same gospel he had preached. We prayed that amongst those we had witnessed to there might be another Gypsy Smith. This is the man who said, "I didn't go to colleges and seminaries. They would not have me. But I have been to the feet of Jesus, where the only true scholarship is learned."

Years later, when I was in Ingleton, we had a Spanish pastor staying with us who had ministered amongst gypsies. It was June and a number of gypsies had set up camp down the road in Bentham after travelling back from Appleby. The Spanish pastor had a real rapport with the gypsies and we had an interesting afternoon as we went from caravan to caravan.

The first Saturday in June was Carnival Day in Morecambe, and each year we had a regular open air witness. To the consternation of our fellow workers, Pat and I chose to get married on Saturday 3rd June, 1972. One young man on his way to attend our wedding was commandeered and never got to the church. Instead, he spent the afternoon witnessing to the crowds on the promenade. Pat was thankful that I opted for the church and not the promenade!

The effects of the 'swinging sixties' began to be seen in the moral and spiritual decline of the seventies: school-sponsored walks on a Sunday; blasphemous films at the cinema; a spiritualist convention at a local theatre; and a homosexual gathering on the Central Pier. These were just some of the events at which we made a stand for truth and righteousness. Sadly, some forty years later most of these things are now well established in our nation.

Saturday afternoons in September and October were often spent on the Golden Mile at Blackpool, mingling with the thousands who had travelled to the resort to see the illuminations. This was before Blackpool became a centre for hen and stag parties, but even in the 1970s we witnessed much drunkenness and lewd behaviour.

Every Saturday night we preached outside The Brunswick Club, where queues assembled for the evening entertainment. Many never gained admission, either because they didn't have the required document or because the club was full. It was a good weekly opportunity to remind the crowds that heaven was not full, but also an opportunity to urge them not to take entrance to heaven for granted. Repentance towards God and faith towards Jesus Christ were the necessary requirements.

Was the open air ministry fruitful? Undoubtedly it is true that often we were 'casting pearls before swine' and yet it was rare that we did not have some profitable discussion. My name and address were always on the gospel leaflets I distributed as well as an offer of free booklets. A number of enquirers responded, and I specifically remember Pat and I being able to give spiritual help to two elderly sisters from Ramsbottom. A friendship developed and we later met when they came to visit us in Morecambe.

Having preached one Sunday afternoon on the promenade at Morecambe, I got into conversation with a lady who had been a Jehovah's Witness for thirty-five years. She told me that she believed the Bible, but I questioned her as to whether it was the Bible or the Watchtower interpretation of the Bible.

We began to speak about the Second Coming of Christ and I challenged her to put the Watchtower material on one side and to read 1 and 2 Thessalonians. We parted on good terms and I heard no more for almost eighteen months, after which she unexpectedly turned up at the church I was attending. She had been truly converted, and having left the Jehovah's Witnesses, she now wished to belong to a true Bible-believing church. As she had read 1 and 2 Thessalonians, she had come to see that the return of Christ could not be something which had already happened in secret but was something visible and audible that was still to happen in the future. This made her question other Jehovah's Witnesses doctrine and caused her, at great personal cost, to sever all contact with the cult.

Open air preaching proved to be a good training ground for the pastorate, and on moving to Ingleton in 1979 it did not altogether come to an end. On Sunday afternoons in August, weather permitting, we had open air meetings in the Community Centre car park in Ingleton. Not an ideal location as on some busy Sundays it was like preaching on the hard shoulder of the motorway.

Was it worthwhile? I cannot point to anyone who was converted but there were other benefits. The open air meeting was always well supported by members of the church, and this meant that believers were 'nailing their colours to the mast' in front of their neighbours and friends. There were also occasions when visitors to Ingleton came to the evening service because of contact made in the afternoon.

Open air work has always been dear to my heart and I read the quarterly Open Air Mission magazine with prayerful interest. It has never been an easy work but I suspect that with every passing year it is getting more difficult. There have and always will be those who are offended by the gospel message, but in the past preaching it was not viewed as a hate crime. Today that is not the case, and it is not uncommon for an open air preacher to be approached or even arrested by the police because of some perceived offensive remark.

I am not suggesting that every open air preacher is innocent and 'preaching the truth in love'. Sadly, I have met a small number of men who have been aggressive, confrontational and provocative. It is not surprising that some of them have been reported to the police. As most open air preachers are godly men with a burden for the lost, it is a great shame that their faithful ministry can be undermined by the behaviour of a few.

I would not pretend to be guiltless myself, as I am sure there were times when I responded to the blasphemies and obscenities of men more with the spirit of James and John (Luke 9:54) than with the Spirit of Christ. It is not always easy to 'hate the sin and love the sinner', and we need to be constantly reminded that "we do not wrestle against flesh and blood, but against principalities, against powers, against the rulers of the darkness of this age, against spiritual hosts of wickedness in the heavenly places" (Ephesians 6:12, NKJV).

CHAPTER FOUR

Unexpected Happenings

HAVING PREACHED OVER FIVE DECADES, it is inevitable that over the years a number of amusing and not too amusing incidents have taken place. I have never been in the RAF but every preacher has to be a member of the RFA – Ready For Anything – for you can never be quite certain what will happen when you go out to preach.

I have always enjoyed taking Harvest Thanksgiving services in country chapels but they have not been without their trickier moments. During the opening prayer on one Sunday morning at Soulby in Cumbria, I felt something on my hand. I half opened an eye and there before me was a wasp. I shook my hand but the wasp was in no hurry to change location. For several seconds my mind was not on what I was praying, but I trust the Lord forgave me for being distracted.

It was at another village Harvest Thanksgiving service that I had a most awkward experience. It was a Monday evening, the church was packed and prior to the service I went to the toilet. To my consternation, I found that the zip on my trousers had gone. This caused no problem whilst I was in the pulpit, but when I shook hands at the door all I could do was fasten my jacket and hope that it would cover my embarrassment.

One Sunday afternoon I went to preach at a village chapel I had never preached at before. I found the building without any difficulty but when I walked inside, half the roof was missing! I followed some ladies who were walking to the village hall. It was here that the service was being held. No one had thought to inform me that the church was out of use for several weeks.

One summer evening I was preaching at the Gospel Hall in Barnoldswick. It had been a scorching day and so the door of the church was left open. During my sermon a dog walked up the aisle, wagging its tail, and had to be escorted off the premises. Recounting the incident to a friend that evening, he commented that the wagging tail probably indicated the dog was charismatic!

One July morning I was preaching at Reads Avenue Baptist Church in Blackpool when, halfway through the sermon, the door opened and a woman walked in. She sat down but almost immediately began to comment or to ask questions about what I was saying. I entered into dialogue with her for a few moments but then suggested that we talked at the end of the service. Not an easy situation and, as I suspected, she was seeking money rather than the truth.

The mention of money reminds me of an amusing incident concerning preaching expenses. At the end of a Bible study I was given an envelope which on the front, thanked me for my ministry. I put it in my pocket and opened it later when I got home. Inside the envelope, despite an intensive search, I found nothing. Pat kindly commented, "Perhaps that is what your Bible study was worth!"

A few weeks later I had a phone call from an embarrassed treasurer who was having difficulty balancing the books. Before he went into any detail, I was able to tell him that I was the answer to his 'problem', and since then we have often laughed about the incident.

Afternoon services in country chapels were often a challenge, as farmers battled with drowsiness. This was understandable as they had been up early and out in the fresh air. Not surprising, therefore, that especially at lambing or hay time, the warmth of the chapel induced sleep. On one occasion I feared for the safety of a middle-aged farmer. He was sound asleep but leaning so much to one side that there was a real danger he might end up on the floor. At the door this man then thanked me for my message. I was tempted to ask which of the three points he had found most helpful.

As a visiting preacher, I have invariably been treated with warmth and affection – but there have been rare exceptions. I arrived at one church to be greeted by the pastor who asked, "What are you doing here?" The appointment had been made by the church secretary several months previously but it was obvious that no one was expecting me. The pastor himself was due to take the service and he appeared most reluctant to stand down. However, having travelled quite a distance and with the mistake being theirs and not mine, I felt that I was fully justified in wanting to fulfil the appointment. I suggested to him that he could lead the service and I would preach. This he rather grudgingly agreed to, but then, after the service commenced at 6pm, it was some fifty-five minutes later before he handed over to me. A few days later I received a letter from one of the deacons at the church, apologising for the behaviour of the pastor. We all have days when our conduct falls short of what it ought to be – perhaps the pastor was just having one of those days!

I always associate preaching with the birth of my son, Andrew. Pat had gone into hospital on Thursday with high blood pressure but I could not visit her on the Friday night as I was preaching at Emmot's Chapel, Wyresdale, near Lancaster. We were not on the telephone, and early the next morning I was awakened by my father-in-law with the news that our first child had been born. As I visited Pat on the Saturday evening, I told her it would be Monday before I saw her again, as I was preaching on Sunday at Hellifield in North Yorkshire.

I took the morning service, had lunch and then to my surprise, my host said, "We are now going to see Pat and the baby." Brian put me in his car and keeping – I think – within the speed limits, we raced to the Queen Victoria Hospital in Morecambe. What a surprise it was for Pat as we spent this unexpected time together. It was then full speed back to Hellifield in order to take the evening service.

When Andrew was three or four, I was taking a farmhouse service and preaching on Enoch. Every time I mentioned the Bible character, Andrew tapped on the kitchen table and said, "E-noch, E-noch." I think the congregation was more amused than I was, but I supposed it showed that Andrew was listening.

Jesus said, "Suffer little children to come unto me," and it is always a joy to see boys and girls in a service; but their presence can be a challenge to the preacher. One Sunday afternoon I was preaching in a village chapel in rural Lancashire and I found myself competing with three or four screaming, crying babies. The older children had gone out to Sunday School but there was no crèche for babies and very young children. I am afraid it was no contest, with the babies easily coming out on top.

I must confess that I was somewhat aggrieved, as I feel it is not fair on the preacher or the congregation and, ultimately, is an insult to God Himself. Should the worship of God and the preaching of His Word be constantly interrupted by children, far too young to understand what is expected of them in church? Surely, it is better for all concerned if churches provide facilities for babies and children too young for Sunday school.

Perhaps such facilities could also cater for breastfeeding mothers! One Sunday afternoon I was preaching at a village in North Yorkshire and a baby began to cry and whimper. The mother took the child out of his carry cot and began to breastfeed him. It had the desired effect, but in no way am I suggesting that all the cries of rural Lancashire should have been settled in the same way.

Older people can also present the preacher with a dilemma. I recall perhaps half a dozen occasions when a person has been taken ill during a service. In most instances it was nothing more than a person fainting because of the heat or because they were suffering from low blood pressure. To stop the service makes the patient the focus of attention and some have been greatly embarrassed afterwards; but not to stop the service makes the preacher appear unfeeling and could, of course, be potentially dangerous if the illness is serious.

There are, however, times when it is the preacher who does not feel well. In general, my experience has been that if I have not felt well at the start of a service, I have felt so much better by the time the service has ended. As I have preached the Word, I have been strengthened both physically and spiritually. The only exception I can remember is one Sunday before a hernia operation, when the pain became so intense that I was sweating profusely. I managed, somehow, to get to the end of the sermon, but had to sit down whilst the closing hymn was sung.

One Saturday afternoon, watching cricket, I fell down an embankment and tore some tendons in my shoulders. A visit to the infirmary resulted in my arm being placed in a sling. This was to prove rather amusing when the next morning I entered the pulpit at

Ingleton to continue my series from Ephesians 6 on... Christian warfare!

It has never been my policy to preach the same sermon twice on a Sunday, but one August Sunday I decided to do so. It had been a busy week and having preached the sermon at Ingleton in the morning, I took it down the road to Clapham in the evening. As I entered the pulpit, my eyes fixed on a family who, on holiday in the area, had worshipped at Ingleton in the morning. What a dilemma! I eventually decided I could not preach the same sermon again. I had no other sermon notes with me, but the Lord was gracious and I managed to get through, although the closing hymn was not altogether appropriate.

Something not too dissimilar was to occur a few years later. I arrived at a church near Keighley to be met by a couple who are in membership with us in Kendal. They were on holiday in the area and did not know that I was the appointed preacher. I remembered that a few weeks earlier at Kendal, David and Helen had heard me preach the sermon I was intending to preach that morning. On finding out they would not be at the evening service, I switched sermons and preached in the morning what I had intended to preach in the evening. Other than having to liaise with the pianist, this did not cause any great problem.

I have always kept a record of sermons and where I have preached them, and so, as far as I know, I have never preached the same sermon at a church twice. However, with there being itinerant congregations as well as itinerant preachers, it is inevitable that some have heard the same sermon twice – or even more.

This is likely to be on the increase in the future, as more and more churches put sermons on their websites. Consequently, I understand that certain well known preachers now request their sermons not to be put on websites. Personally, I can see that website sermons are of great benefit for those who are housebound, but otherwise I feel such sermons can never fully recapture the spirit in which they were first preached.

CHAPTER FIVE

Pastoral Preaching

ONE SUNDAY EVENING IN AUGUST 1976, I was preaching at Ingleton Evangelical Church, and in the congregation there were two experienced pastors on holiday – Rev. Peter Secombe and Rev. Derek Swann. Neither man was known to me, but afterwards, as we shook hands at the door, one of them said, "I think you should be in the ministry." I thought nothing more of this passing remark until almost three years later, when I was approached by the elders from that church, asking me to prayerfully consider becoming their pastor. Coincidence? I do not think so; the Lord, in His providence, was confirming that this call was indeed from Him.

There were other confirmations as well. The elders from Ingleton first came to see me on a Thursday evening – the night Margaret Thatcher came to power – and the next morning I was back at work in the Jobcentre. Around midday I had a phone call, the like of which I had never had before. A man was telling me that he had taken an overdose of tablets and he wished to see me before he died. I telephoned an ambulance and then rushed to the man's home. As I travelled along Morecambe promenade, this happening seemed to be far more than coincidence. It served to confirm what the Ingleton elders had put to me the night before; I was being called to the pastoral ministry. Thankfully the man survived.

Confirmation was needed, as a number of believers were advising me not to risk the security of the Civil Service for the uncertainty of a rural pastorate. Having a wife and two young children, I appreciate that their advice was given with the very best of motives, and we would not have moved forward without the inner conviction that this was the will of God.

Thus began thirty years of preaching to the same congregation. Initially, this was a new discipline as, in addition to other responsibilities, two sermons had to be prepared each week. The Lord certainly undertook for me. Although sometimes the ink was only just dry on the paper, there was always a sermon ready for when it was required.

In 1979 the congregation was small, but visitors swelled the numbers in the summer months. It was not unusual for well-known preachers to be in the congregation but, thankfully, it was only after the service that I found out who they were. They were unfailingly kind, and friendships made over thirty years ago continue to the present time.

One July morning there was an unusual visitor to the church. The previous evening we had been disturbed just before midnight by a knock at our door and a man declaring, "I'm an evangelical." On opening the door, we were confronted by a tramp wanting something to eat and a bed for the night. Pat made him a meal and I took him down to the church, where I had a pillow and duvet for such visitors.

I went back to the church at 8.30am and my friend was snoring loudly. He came back for breakfast and I promised him a Sunday roast, provided he attended the morning service. Thus it was that this unkempt 'man of the road' came to be sat at the back of the church. I was heartened by the way he was received by the congregation – no need to preach from James 2 that morning.

Many different kinds of churches go under the name 'evangelical' and this was reflected in the visitors to the church. Remarkably, I can only recall one awkward moment in those thirty years. We had sung the closing hymn and I was about to pronounce the benediction, when a woman began to speak in tongues. I considered it then, and still do, a most inappropriate intervention, as it must have been obvious to her that we were not a charismatic church. One of the positive things about the advent of church websites is that visitors are now able to know the stance of a holiday church before they even walk through the doors.

Baptismal services were always a special occasion, and in the goodness of the Lord there were very few years when we did not have such services. During my early years in Ingleton we had to use other churches' baptisteries, and whilst grateful for their support, it did present its own problems. At one church there was so little water in the baptistery that I was in danger of wrenching my back as I lifted the person back up out of the water, whilst at another church we rejected the black baptismal gowns as they looked as though they might have been owned by Noah.

In 1985 we built a baptistry within the church, and it was a memorable evening when it was used for the very first time. Among the candidates there was a man in his seventies who had been wonderfully converted when Paul Bassett, from Melbourne Hall, Leicester, preached at our Harvest Mission. Another candidate for baptism was a lady in her sixties, who had a phobic fear of water but she was determined to be baptised by total immersion. Memorable days.

Not all who were baptised were new converts, as a number from a Methodist background were mature Christians, christened as babies but not totally immersed as believers. One lady in her eighties, a believer for many years, requested baptism and it was most encouraging to see someone of that age responding to the Word. For reasons of age and health, she was baptised by effusion rather than total immersion, but again, it was a precious occasion.

Preaching brought the joy of seeing believers being built up and encouraged in the faith, but the greatest joy was seeing unbelievers coming to faith through the preaching of the gospel.

Alison was a sixteen-year-old girl spending part of her summer holidays with one of our elders and his wife. As the gospel was preached one Sunday evening, the Lord opened her heart and she was truly converted. And thirty-five years later I was to meet her son, Caleb, a student at Lancaster University, playing the piano at an evangelical church in the city. When the gospel is preached and someone is converted, we never know the impact that might have upon future generations.

The first convert we were to see in Ingleton was a man with no church background but addicted to gambling on the horses. Not every conversion is dramatic but Ted's was. His mother was our next door neighbour and one summer evening Pat, in a quiet way, shared the gospel with him. That night Ted had a vision of Jesus; his desire to gamble was taken away and he became a new creature in Christ! His testimony appeared in Challenge newspaper and Ted has continued to walk with the Lord throughout many testing circumstances.

Ted knew that I had been baptised in the sea at Morecambe, and with the church baptistry not yet having been built, he requested a similar baptism. We had to check the tide times but one lovely afternoon Ted was baptised beneath the waves. It was a wonderful gospel opportunity, for as crowds gathered on the promenade, we were able to share with them the significance of what was taking place.

His son Geoff saw the change in his dad but, being fond of the drink, had no desire to change. This continued for ten years, until his grandmother died. Mrs Richardson was eighty-nine and Geoff thought the world of his grandmother. She had had a hard life and, though not professing to be a believer, there were many things which were most commendable about her.

At her funeral service, I mentioned these things but I never said that she had or had not gone to heaven. 'The Lord knows those who are His' – we are not the judge of anyone. The following Sunday, Geoff was at both services and his attendance continued, with Geoff eventually telling me that he had come to faith in Christ.

When I asked him what had happened, I was amazed at his answer: "At my grandmother's funeral you did not say that she had gone to heaven. And the thought came to me that if a good woman like my grandmother had perhaps not gone to heaven, what hope was there for me?" This was the sovereignty of God. I have known relatives angry when pastors have not said that their loved one was in heaven, but Geoff was not angry, he was anxious, and it was this which caused him to seek the Lord. The sovereignty of God in salvation is amazing. He saved someone not through what I said but through what I did not say. Geoff became a deacon in the church and served faithfully until his sudden home call in 2011.

On door-to-door visitation I met a retired lady who was always most eager to discuss the Bible and spiritual matters. She had a church background but found it difficult to believe that salvation could only be accomplished through the death of Jesus. To her, this made Christianity rather a bloodthirsty faith.

In the providence of God, she moved into a house almost next to the church and began to join us for worship on a Sunday morning. Sometime later, she began to attend the Wednesday night Bible study and I 'happened' to be going through the Book of Galatians. In this epistle, Paul's great argument is that salvation is only through faith in the sacrificial death of Jesus – nothing more, nothing less, nothing else.

One Thursday afternoon I went to see Mrs P. and she excitedly told me, "I see it! I see it!" In the Bible study she had indeed come to see that not only was the death of Jesus necessary for our salvation, it was the only thing that was necessary for our salvation. Mrs P. became a committed member of the church and served faithfully until she had to move into a nursing home.

Teenagers, gamblers, respectable church attenders – the gospel of Christ "is the power of God to salvation for everyone who believes" (Romans 1:16, NKJV). What a joy it was to see the reality of this in people of different ages and with very different backgrounds. Truly, it is not only the angels in heaven who rejoice when sinners repent.

It was my custom to preach consecutively through a book of the Bible on Sunday mornings and Wednesday evenings. This system has much to commend it, bringing as it does the 'whole counsel of God' to the attention of preacher and congregation. It also saves the preacher from majoring on his particular 'hobby horse' and means no one can accuse him of just choosing a particular verse, or verses, in order to get at them.

I always considered some books more suitable for a Sunday morning and others more suitable for a Wednesday evening. This was especially so as, with being in a holiday area, on many Sunday mornings there were visitors in the congregation. It was important that they should benefit from the sermon, even though they had not been present on previous weeks. I also felt it was important not to get too bogged down and to move through books at a reasonable pace. I know Dr Martyn Lloyd-Jones spent thirteen years preaching through the Book of Romans and only got to chapter 14, but I am no Martyn Lloyd-Jones!

As a young preacher, I had the privilege of being introduced to the man himself when he preached at Banks Methodist Church, Southport. His books and tapes were a tremendous help to me and he very much influenced my ministry. Whatever movements arose or bandwagons were passing, 'The Doctor' just continued faithfully preaching the Word. This is what I was determined to do at Ingleton and the Lord undoubtedly blessed us as He strengthened and built up the church.

One of the advantages of being an independent church minister is that, generally, the majority of the congregation are sympathetic to your preaching ministry. This is not always the case in other denominations. A vicar recounted to me how in one of his churches, when he started to preach, a man always removed his hearing aid and held it aloft. It was not replaced until he was announcing the last hymn.

In 1983 I suggested that we had an annual Bible Convention, and this was held on the first Saturday in June for the next twenty-five years. It was known as the Yorkshire Dales Bible Convention and attracted believers from all over the north of England.

In some ways the first convention was the most memorable: principally, for the Spirit-anointed preaching of Rev. Peter Jeffrey of Rugby, but also for the extreme weather conditions. It was a scorching hot day, but during the evening meeting the clouds gathered and there was a violent thunderstorm. Such was the torrential rain that my brother and his wife opted to stay the night rather than travel back to their holiday caravan in Cumbria. It was a wise decision, as throughout the night there was further thunder, lightning and heavy rain.

I was always grateful to busy men who were prepared to make long journeys in order to preach at the convention. A few stayed overnight and preached on the Sunday, but most travelled back many miles to be in their own pulpits. I remember with affection men such as Hywel Jones, Paul Brown, Gareth Crossley, Errol Hulse, Paul Bassett, Neil Richards, Brian Edwards, and we look to the Lord to again raise up a similar generation of preachers.

CHAPTER SIX

'A Little Child Shall Lead Them' – The Ministry of Aaron

PAT AND I HAD BECOME foster carers in 1986, and eighteen months later we had a telephone call from Social Services. A baby born to drug-addicted parents had been battered by his father and there was now a desperate need for a foster home. Thus it was, at ten weeks old, Aaron came into our lives.

"You have not destroyed him but you have destroyed any possibility of him ever having a normal life." These were the words of the judge as Aaron's father was sentenced to six years in prison. It was a November afternoon when we picked Aaron up from the hospital and the words of the paediatrician were not very encouraging: "Are you sure you know what you are taking on?" Having had little experience of handicapped children, we did *not* know what we were taking on, but having sought the Lord, we knew it was the right thing to do.

The first two months were the most difficult as Aaron cried day and night. This was cerebral crying, not the normal crying of a baby, and it was impossible to placate him. Our own two children were fourteen and ten at the time and we were conscious of our responsibilities towards them. In the goodness of God, they both accepted Aaron into our home and immediately treated him as their brother.

Initially, Aaron came to us for one year, but having got 'his feet under the table' he became a well-loved member of our family and in April, 2004 we adopted him. Life with a multi-handicapped child has often proved challenging and yet there have been positives we could never have envisaged when Aaron first came to us.

We have been invited to speak about Aaron at ladies' meetings, coffee mornings, church lunches and youth groups. Amongst teenagers we have stressed that Aaron is the tragic consequence of what drug-taking can lead to and we trust the sight of a severely disabled young man will act as a deterrent to any who might be tempted to experiment with drugs. Satan often takes us further than we want to go, and experimentation can end in addiction.

At other meetings we have shared the many things that our years with Aaron have taught us. As a result of the Fall, Cain killed his brother and men continue to inflict pain and death upon family members. The effects of the Fall are still tragically with us because man's innate nature has not changed.

When Aaron was twelve months old, we had a visit from his paternal grandparents. My heart went out to them, as I saw a couple distressed and devastated by what their son had done to a child. John Donne said, "No man is an island," and how true that is. The good or the bad we do has an impact upon other people.

Aaron can do nothing for himself and is dependent on us and others for his needs to be met. This is a daily reminder to us of our own dependence upon the Lord for all our needs, both material and spiritual. It is in Him that "we live and move and have our being" (Acts 17:28, NKJV) and it is to Him that we must look for our eternal salvation.

This is a hard world, but would it not be even harder if everyone was strong in body and sound in mind? Time and again we have seen how Aaron has brought the best out in other people. So often it is ones such as Aaron who melt human hearts and enable us to see that men are still made in the image of God. We have been the recipients of great kindness and generosity, as the hearts of believers and unbelievers have been touched by Aaron.

During our years in the pastorate, we came to see what an asset Aaron was in the work of evangelism. People who initially were not sympathetic to the gospel we preached were more sympathetic to us because of him. This meant doors were opened which otherwise might have remained shut.

Aaron's adoption provided us with another gospel theme. Fostering is an excellent thing but there is nothing permanent about it. In theory, Aaron could have been taken from us at any time during the sixteen years he was fostered. This all changed at adoption, when that which was a temporary arrangement became permanent. Aaron now has our name, our address and – for what it is worth – our wealth.

How much more wonderful to be adopted into the family of God! No solicitor or social worker is necessary, as it is all through God's grace. The transaction is done when we come to faith in His Son, the Lord Jesus Christ. We receive His name – we are called Christians. Heaven, His home, becomes our home. And we become "heirs of God and joint heirs with Christ" (Romans 8:17, NKJV). How amazing to be the adopted sons and daughters of Almighty God!

People are often saddened when they see the extent of Aaron's disabilities, but we are able to set before them the Christian hope: "The Lord Jesus Christ ... will transform our lowly body that it may be conformed to His glorious body..." (Philippians 3:21, NKJV) This is a precious promise and one we believe will be fulfilled in Aaron. Our bodies are going to be redeemed, and in the new heaven and the new earth Aaron will be able to do all those things which on earth he cannot do.

We have a God who is able to bring good out of evil. This was supremely demonstrated at the cross. Evil men did their worst but through the death of Christ multitudes have been redeemed and brought into the family of God. It is not easy to understand the sufferings of any child but we can testify that in Aaron God has brought good out of evil. We have been encouraged and challenged by him, and as we have told his story we trust many others have as well.[1]

[1] Aaron, after a short illness, went to be with the Lord on 18th May, 2016.

CHAPTER SEVEN

Suffer the Children to Come unto Me

DURING MOST SUMMERS IN THE 1970s I took a week off work to help with Morecambe's Children Hour. This meeting had been started by Keith Bowers, a chemistry master at Morecambe Grammar School, and met every weekday morning in August on the giant steps opposite the Winter Gardens. Keith had a loudspeaker system attached to his van and every morning we would tour the town, advertising the meeting. Those were the days when families were still spending a week or two at the Morecambe seaside and there would be children present from all over the country.

There was the usual mix of action choruses, quizzes, memory texts and Bible stories. Often parents or grandparents stayed with their children and we were conscious of this when applying the Bible stories. The weather generally seemed to be favourable, but when it was wet we met in the Clarence Street Gospel Hall. It was in the Gospel Hall that at the end of one meeting an Irish man accepted a Gospel. When Jim returned with his two children the following year, he was a 'new creature' in Christ and he faithfully served the Lord until his death a few years ago.

When we came to Ingleton in 1979, the Wednesday Special children's meeting was already well established, and Pat and I were to be involved in this meeting until retirement in 2009. The children ranged in age from three to eleven, and on some Wednesday evenings forty children would be in attendance. With the passing of the years, parents who themselves had been in Wednesday Special were now bringing their children to the meeting.

I picked some of the children up in my own car and I dare not think how many youngsters were sometimes packed into the vehicle! It was in the days before seatbelts and booster seats, when risk assessment was just in its infancy. This meant we could take the children to Morecambe and to the top of Ingleborough without having to satisfy the Health and Safety lobby. Despite the absence of red tape, we valued every child and their safety was always our prime consideration.

In the early 1980s, we had an inter-church quiz with Bethel Chapel, Clapham. There were four children of similar age on each team and I was the question setter and quizmaster. Each child had a buzzer, and though not quite as professional as Top of the Form or University Challenge, it was always a hard-fought competition. A trophy was presented to the winning team and was held by them for a year.

Egg-rolling was an annual Easter event at Nutstile Farm and a nativity play was always presented at Christmas. Pat produced the nativity play and one year, unknown to her, the shepherds were accompanied by a real sheep. The sheep was rather startled by being in a church full of people, but not as startled as Pat!

May saw the Wednesday Special prizegiving service. Originally it was held on a Wednesday evening but later it changed to a Sunday morning. The church was packed with children, parents and grandparents, and it was a good gospel opportunity. It was quite a logistical exercise to ensure that every child got a book, and not one that they had already received. An older member of the church was chosen to present the books.

There are believers today who would testify that it was at Wednesday Special that they came to saving faith in Christ. The meeting was, however, not just an outreach to children. For example, a lady called Peggy brought her grandchildren to the meetings and as a result started to attend the evening service. Sometime later she was converted, baptised and became a faithful member of the church. Some years afterwards her husband also came to faith and was received into church membership.

There were other benefits too, which we recently discovered. A quiz was being held at one of the clubs in Ingleton and, to the surprise of everyone, a lady was able to answer a question from the Bible. When asked,

"How do you know that?" her answer was, "Aunty Pat and Wednesday Special."

Wednesday Specials were not without their humorous and ironical moments over the years. For example, when asked what an idol was, a young girl answered, "Someone who will not work." And a leader confessed to losing her temper with a group of girls whilst teaching them the fruit of the Spirit – long-suffering, kindness, gentleness and self-control!

Sometimes we were asked how we managed to get so many children to the meetings. The implication was that there might be a 'secret formula', but there was no secret to it – just hard work. There were times when other activities for children were started in Ingleton on a Wednesday evening, but we were determined to make Wednesday Special so 'special' that we would be able to compete with other attractions. Due to the loyalty of parents and the hard work of helpers, this objective was achieved.

For the first two years I was at Ingleton, I did a children's talk in the morning service. This was a rewarding but also daunting commitment, as preparing for children can sometimes be more challenging than preparing for adults. Things changed due to a fortnight's holiday in Wales in the summer of 1981. At that time I holidayed from Saturday to Saturday, but eventually I found this was not a wise move as it meant coming back to two services the next day. Feeling pressurised, Pat offered to do the children's talk and, having done it that once, she continued to give the talks until I retired.

More often than not when I am taking a service, Pat still does the talk for the children. I feel it is so important that speakers should be able to communicate with the children and Pat does this better than me. Having heard children's talks on 'Artificial Insemination' and 'How to Remove Warts from Cows' Udders', I realise this is not an area in which every preacher is gifted!

Some take exception to a woman teaching in a service, and I am in full agreement with this scriptural position. However, I maintain that Pat is teaching the children not the adults, though it is not unusual for the children's talk to be better received by the adults than the sermon!

Aaron attended a PMLD[2] school near Carnforth, and for a number of years I was on the governing body. This brought me into contact with parents and consequently there were occasions when, sadly, a child died and I was asked to officiate at the funeral. These were always emotionally draining services but I was pleased to be able to offer some help and comfort.

When David's baby died, he said, "I shall go to him, but he shall not return to me." (2 Samuel 12:23, KJV) As David's eternal destiny was "the house of the Lord forever" (Psalm 23:6, KJV), we can deduce from this that his baby was already in the presence of the Lord. This is my conviction concerning babies and all who do not have the mental capacity to understand the gospel. They are, I believe, covered by the blood of Christ. For

[2] Profound and Multiple Learning Disabilities

this reason, I was able to hold out the gospel hope to grieving parents and relatives.

Because Sunday schools have declined and there is now little or no Bible teaching in day schools, today's children are being brought up ignorant of the Scriptures and of the gospel. This means we are increasingly in a missionary situation, for without some knowledge of the Bible the Holy Spirit is working in a vacuum. There is no scriptural truth that He can apply to the heart.

This is a depressing fact, as we become more and more a pagan nation, and yet, perhaps, there is a positive aspect. How often I have heard this from people of my generation: "I had it forced down my throat when I was a youngster." Sometimes I think the 'Christian' teaching they received as youngsters just gave them an immunity to the real thing.

As present-day children develop into adulthood, they will not be able to make such an accusation. The Christian faith is not being forced upon them – it is rather being denied them. This is sad and yet, in the providence of God, it may well present the Church with an exciting opportunity.

Some years ago I got into conversation with some young teenagers in Scarborough and they told me that we had all descended from apes. I expressed ignorance and amazement, as though I had never heard such a thing before, and I pressed them for more information. How did it happen? How long did it take to happen? Was there anyone who made it happen? Where had they got their information from? Their initial confidence gave way to hesitancy, and having had to examine their belief, they were not as dogmatic. Indeed, having set before them the biblical account of creation, they were attentive and respectful. They did not mock and I began to see that I was, perhaps, telling some of them things which they had never heard before. This will increasingly be the case in the future and may well provide good gospel opportunities. How we need to pray for children and young people!

CHAPTER EIGHT

Dedications, Marriages and Funerals

IN RURAL, INDEPENDENT evangelical churches, 'hatches, matches and dispatches' are not as routine as they are in a parish church. Though, with the secularisation of our society, even in parish churches these life events are by no means as frequent as they once were. Children are not being christened, weddings are taking place in hotels, and funerals are being increasingly held at the crematorium.

Being by conviction a baptistic church, we did not christen children but instead dedicated them. It was a meaningful service in which we thanked God for the safe arrival of the baby and the parents promised to bring the child up in "the training and instruction of the Lord" (Ephesians 6:4, NIV). As I nursed them, most of the babies were on their best behaviour – some apparently fascinated by a man with a beard.

It was a special joy to be able to take part in the dedication of our five grandchildren. Saul and Elodie were dedicated at Chapel Allerton Baptist Church in Leeds, whilst Reuben, Rose and Elsie were dedicated at Billingham Baptist Church. They are our grandchildren but we pray that one day they will become the adopted sons and daughters of Almighty God.

One morning a desperate grandmother called to see me. Her unmarried daughter had given birth to a girl but the mother had no intention of having the child christened. "What will happen," begged the grandmother, "if the baby dies without ever being christened?" I explained that as a church we did not christen children and that I did not believe the eternal welfare of a baby would ever be determined by a ritual the child was not even aware of. I hope I was able to reassure the woman, but how sad that she should be tormented by a manmade tradition.

Shortly after I came to Ingleton the church was registered for weddings. This was quite a laborious process, as a certain number of people had to confirm that the building was their regular place of worship and a secure safe had also to be obtained. Prior to this the registrar had to be present at the service or the couple had to get married at the register office before the wedding ceremony at the church.

Almost without exception, weddings were joyful occasions and I have many happy memories. That is not to say they were never stressful. One is anxious that no mishap should spoil the big day, and with cameras now filming every movement, the pressure is even greater.

The only negativity I experienced was when some feminist friends of a bride took exception to my exposition of Ephesians 5, which teaches that husbands must love their wives and wives should submit to their husbands. Perhaps my exposition was not as clear as it should have been – or it might have been that word 'submit'!

I always felt it necessary to give an address at a wedding but I must confess, I never found it easy. Lengthy sermons were inappropriate and yet it was important to say something significant and meaningful. I suppose the excitement and busyness of the day is not altogether conducive to attentive listening.

My son Andrew married Sarah at Kirk Levington Parish Church near Yarm in 2007 and I was invited to address the happy couple. This was followed, just three months later, by my daughter Joanna's marriage to Alan at Gayle Methodist Church. The service was led by my brother, as I was otherwise engaged – proudly walking my daughter down the aisle. It turned out to be a poignant occasion as it was the last time I was to see my ninety-four-year-old mother on earth. Two days later she was called into the presence of the Lord.

Funerals were never easy occasions, as often you were officiating at the service of someone you loved and knew well. I always considered it important to keep my own emotions in check during the service, but I sometimes felt emotionally drained afterwards. It is true that funerals present gospel opportunities but I never took advantage of the situation, hopefully preaching the 'truth in love' and with sensitivity.

I felt it was of the utmost importance to make every service personal. This came home to me when I stood at a lectern at the crematorium. On the lectern there was a piece of paper with these words written on it: "Husband died in war. Fond of cats." I presume the rota minister at the previous funeral had never known the lady and this was the scant information provided by the family or undertaker.

This reminded me of attending the funeral of a work colleague in the 1970s and how, throughout the service, the minister kept getting his name wrong. How sad to come to the end of life and to have such an impersonal service. Even when I did not know a person well, it was my custom to visit the family and glean as much information as I possibly could.

'They ministered to me far more than I ministered to them' might be an old cliché, but this was invariably true when I visited terminally ill patients. Again and again I was moved by their courage in suffering and challenged by their confident hope in the face of death. They were witnesses to the truth of the 23rd Psalm: "Yea, though I walk through the valley of the shadow of death, I will fear no evil. For You are with me; Your rod and Your staff, they comfort me." (NKJV)

I am thankful that I was able to speak at the funeral services of my father-in-law, my mother-in-law and also my brother, Ken. These services were at Heysham Free Methodist Church and though I was emotional, His grace was sufficient. My mother's funeral service was also held at the same church but to speak on that occasion would have been a step too far.

I hesitate to mention amusing incidents at funerals, as I have no desire to detract from the solemnity of the occasion. When a football supporter I knew collapsed and died at a match, a coach was laid on by the club to take fans from the stadium to the crematorium. Fans were encouraged to wear their football shirts, scarves and hats in order to give the deceased 'a good send-off'. This, sadly, is the spirit of the age and should not be encouraged.

However, one day I was conducting a funeral service at the crematorium and the last hymn was 'When I Survey the Wondrous Cross'. There was no organist present but the crematorium official assured me he had the music on tape and we could sing to the recording. There were no more than twenty-five mourners at the service, but the tape was of a Welsh choir of a hundred voices. Anyone walking by must have been transfixed by the heavenly sound coming from the crematorium that morning! And yet, even that – beautiful as it was – is just a feeble foretaste of the worship of heaven, where "in a nobler, sweeter song, we shall sing His power to save".

CHAPTER NINE

Miscellaneous Times and Venues

I HAVE ALWAYS BEEN AN 'early to bed, early to rise' kind of person but whether this has made me 'healthy, wealthy and wise' is debatable. I mention this because I had to take a watchnight service on New Year's Eve at Ingleton for a number of years. Certainly a challenge to my body clock!

On the first occasion it was mince pies at 11pm, followed by the service at 11.30pm. This meant a sleepy pastor leaving a warm house, going out on a frosty night and eating *yet more* mince pies. I do not remember the service but I do remember the evening, howbeit not for the best of reasons.

Subsequent years were much better, as we had a church social prior to the watchnight service. We had good food and good fun and then, together as a church family, we 'praised Him for all that was past and trusted Him for all that was to come'. It was a great way in which to end one year and to start the next.

In 1971 I was involved in a different kind of watchnight service. I was attending Heysham Free Methodist Church and as revellers came out of the Strawberry Gardens public house, we invited them to come to the service. It was the first time I had ever preached in the early hours of the morning but several men did come. They were, perhaps surprisingly, quite attentive, but due to the amount of liquid they had consumed, some had to make regular visits to the toilet.

During my time in Ingleton we had monthly meetings at a nursing home and in the sheltered housing complex. We sang well-known hymns and had a prayer and Bible reading before I gave a simple gospel message. There were almost always believers amongst the residents, and whilst we saw the services as an outreach to the elderly, nevertheless they were an encouragement to Christians who could not get to worship services.

Inevitably, due to the age of the people, there were amusing incidents. A couple of elderly residents came to blows on one occasion because one of them was sat in the wrong chair. Another time, a woman requested that we sing, "Bless them all. Bless them all. The long and the short and the tall." Also, it was not unusual to hear, "I wish he'd speak up. What's he saying? I can't hear a word." Speaking to old people and children is generally far more challenging than preaching to a Sunday congregation.

Sadly, I fear that such services might well become a thing of the past. Nursing and old people's homes will increasingly be occupied by a non-churchgoing generation, many of whom will never have sung the old familiar hymns. Permission to hold such services will, I suspect, be more difficult to obtain in the future than it has been in the past.

In the 1970s I attended a service on the locked ward of a psychiatric hospital. As the service proceeded, one of our group was attacked by a disturbed patient – an unnerving experience which made me appreciate the stressful work that mental health staff do, but also how difficult it can be to reach such patients with the gospel. Today there are far fewer psychiatric hospitals and the service we had in the 1970s would not be permitted today.

On several occasions I have been on panels for Question Times at local churches. These have generally been young people's meetings and I have invariably found them stimulating and profitable. In the late 1980s I found myself on a panel that was very different. It was when the A65 Settle bypass was about to be built and an 'eco warriors' group was concerned as to what it would do to the environment.

I am not too sure why I was asked, but I duly took my place with three others – including a town councillor – at Settle Town Hall. Most of the questions centred on the cost and the environmental impact of the development – not, I have to say, my specialist subjects. I remember commenting that we are stewards of God's creation and responsible for what we pass on to future generations, whilst also stressing that the Creator is more important than the creation. To the frustration of the 'eco warriors', the road was built, but remembering how Settle town centre used to be a bottleneck I have always been thankful for the bypass.

Most of my preaching has been in independent evangelical churches but other pulpits have been open to me. Consequently, I have preached in Methodist, Free Methodist, Baptist, Congregational, Church of England, Salvation Army, Church of the Nazarene, Pentecostal and Brethren churches.

In the early 1980s I took part in a service at the Welsh Chapel in Llanymawddy. We were on holiday in the village with my brother and his family and we were asked to take an English-speaking service. It was the chapel where Dr Martyn Lloyd-Jones had often preached and where, some fourteen months previously, he had preached at one of his final services in Wales.

I have also preached in houses, farmhouses, barns, schools, community centres, as well as at the Liberal Rooms, the Labour Club and a St John's Ambulance Hall. Often groups of believers were hiring premises until they were able to have their own church building. Prior to the smoking ban becoming law in 2007, some of these venues still had the smell of stale tobacco, even on a Sunday night.

By contrast, services at farmhouses were usually much more inviting, as tea would sometimes be served in front of a coal fire between services. This reminds me that at Reads Avenue in Blackpool the congregation stayed for lunch between the morning and the afternoon service. I can only hope that good food and fellowship was followed by good preaching.

On one occasion I spoke from a trailer in a barn, when my uncle and I were the preachers at Brookhouse Camp Meeting. Camp meetings originated in North America and were the forerunners of Primitive Methodism in the UK. Based on American revival meetings, they consisted of preaching, prayer, singing and testimonies, and sometimes ended with a fellowship meal known as a love feast.

On five occasions during the 1980s I preached with my brother at a camp meeting in Cumbria. It was the first Sunday in July and the intention was to have the meetings outside, in front of the church. However, we only managed one service outdoors, as three times there was the prospect of rain and another time it was too hot! I was not convinced that they really wanted to be outside.

One Sunday evening I spoke in a farmhouse at an after church gathering for young people. These youngsters were certainly unchurched and it was a challenge to get their attention. However, the farmer and his wife faced a far greater challenge for, having provided food, their kindness was rewarded with some young men throwing sandwiches at each other and with one young man even eating a daffodil! It raised the old dilemma – we want such youngsters to hear the gospel, but when does their behaviour bar them from the meetings?

Young people were generally better behaved when I took school assemblies. Indeed, my problem was not so much with the students but often with the teachers. It was most discouraging to see teachers totally disinterested – even marking books – as the pupils were being addressed. As a visiting speaker invited by the school, it was, if nothing else, a lack of courtesy. What a contrast to my own school days in the 1960s when teachers would reprimand any student who was talking or being disruptive in assembly.

By contrast, I have happier memories of taking the assembly at Bentham Grammar School. This was a boarding school and the assembly was on a Sunday morning. The head teacher had a rota of all the denominations, and he was eager that you should give your particular emphasis. This meant one enjoyed a freedom and could unapologetically present the gospel. An added bonus was that Pat, the children and I were then invited to lunch with the head teacher and the staff.

Paul rejoiced that 'Christ is preached' and I rejoice that whether at midday or midnight, whether in churches, nursing homes, barns or schools, I have had the opportunity to make Christ known. As our society becomes ever more secular, it is questionable whether future generations of preachers will have quite the same opportunities.

CHAPTER TEN

Retirement, Itinerancy and Reflection

IT WAS A GREAT PRIVELEGE to preach to the same congregation for thirty years, but retirement has given me the opportunity to engage in an itinerant ministry.

The difference between a pastoral and an itinerant ministry has been compared to the difference between being a parent and a grandparent. You have the privilege without the responsibility! This is, however, only true up to a point. I do feel a pastoral responsibility whenever I preach, but the ultimate responsibility is, of course, with the pastor of the church.

My itinerant ministry is centred on the north of England but I have strayed as far as Cardiff to take two Christian Endeavour Autumn Conferences. Retirement has also given me the opportunity to take a series of weekly Bible studies at various churches and to be the speaker when churches have had weekends away.

Many churches are without pastors, but it has been a joy to work with a number of them as they have sought to appoint a minister. Some have indeed appointed pastors and my services are not required as once they were. This is one instance when I do not mind putting myself out of work.

One of the joys of itinerancy is the hospitality and fellowship we enjoy with fellow believers. Great kindness has been shown by so many, as homes have been opened to Pat, Aaron and me. The Sunday roasts we have relished have, I am sure, been superior to many served in hotels and restaurants. However, it is not even the meals we are most grateful for but the friendships made, as we have shared our joys and our burdens together.

At some houses I have been offered a bed for an afternoon nap, and when required this has refreshed me for the evening service. This is the opposite to what once happened to my uncle. Having had his Sunday lunch at a farmhouse, he was shown into the front room and he expected his hosts to join him. However, this did not happen for a couple of hours, as the farmer and his wife had gone to bed for the afternoon!

In forty-five years of preaching I have had hospitality in scores of homes and can only ever remember one disappointing experience. Having preached with my brother one afternoon at a harvest thanksgiving service in the Yorkshire Dales, we went with our wives to a house in the village.

"I am sure you don't want to come inside yet," the lady said, "on such a beautiful afternoon. Go for a drive and come back at 5pm." We did as we were told, and when we got back, a most acceptable tea was set before us. The lady, however, did not engage in conversation but sat with her back to us and watched the television. It was the only time I ever felt that we might have been better with sandwiches and a thermos flask!

I have long had an interest in preaching, and in retirement the way has opened up for me to be involved in Preaching Seminars. This initially came about through my friendship with Ron Collard in Ripon. Ron is a retired pastor but also an ex-RAF and Missionary Aviation Fellowship pilot. We were conscious that, especially in independency, men who felt a call to preach were often hampered by the lack of training available. This meant that too often strengths were not encouraged and weaknesses were not addressed. Consequently, we prepared a seminar which covers the following areas:

- the supremacy of preaching in a multimedia society;
- preparation of self;
- preparation of material;
- proclamation and examination.

The first seminar was held in Harrogate in 2014 and was appreciated by the twenty-five preachers who attended. Other such seminars are planned for the future.

Revd George Hemmings – once the assistant to Dr Martyn Lloyd-Jones at Westminster Chapel – was ninety-three when he died. Shortly before his death in 2009 he said to me, "Throughout my ministry, the tide has been going out and it does not show any signs of turning." Sadly, he was right, and over the last fifty years I have seen our country becoming ever more secular.

This is reflected in the number of churches I have preached in which are now closed. I have counted over thirty such churches, but I am sure there are others that I have forgotten. Many are now houses and two have been turned into car parks. Many country churches are just kept going by a faithful, elderly few, so unless there is a heaven-sent revival, I fear it is only a matter of time before more doors are shut.

I remember coming out of a car park in Oswestry once and ahead of me there was a large church building. A banner was on display on the outside and from a distance I thought it said "Sunday Message". However, on getting closer to the building, I discovered the words were not "Sunday Message" but rather "Sunbed Massage". The redundant church was now a health and fitness centre.

It has to be said that a number of churches have closed because of a departure from the truth and a lack of evangelistic zeal. Sadly, for many years they had not been seeking to make disciples and consequently, as an older generation died, the church died with them.

This is not to say that the last forty to fifty years have not had their encouragements. True, churches have closed, but new works have begun and I have preached at over twenty churches that were not in existence in 1970. The Lord has His faithful remnant, and churches which departed from the truth have been replaced by churches seeking a return to biblical doctrines and biblical standards. Many of these are thriving and proving that the gospel of Christ is still "the power of God unto salvation" (Romans 1:16, KJV).

Looking back, I can but thank the Lord for calling me to preach and for putting me into the ministry. When the Lord calls, He provides, and Pat and I can truly testify to the faithfulness of God. All our needs were wonderfully met, occasionally in dramatic ways, but generally through the commitment and the generosity of His people in Ingleton. There were only sixteen members when we arrived in 1979 but no pastor could have asked for a more prayerful and supportive people.

I am sure there are disadvantages to a long pastorate but in my experience the plusses outnumbered the minuses. It takes time, especially in rural areas, for the pastor to be accepted, and also time for the pastor to become acquainted with the distinctive characteristics of the people. In my later years I was increasingly asked to officiate at the funerals of non-churchgoers and this was only because, with the passing of time, I had built up a relationship with them.

That is not to say that in those thirty years the thought of moving never occurred to me. I had tentative approaches from other churches, which had to be considered, but I never felt led to act upon them. However, this was not the case in 1991, when I did feel that perhaps both church and pastor would benefit from a change. I was about to share this with my elders and deacons when two providences stopped me in my tracks.

Conscious that we were an aging congregation, the church had been praying for young families to join us. Most unexpectedly, a young family committed themselves to the church and I did not feel that their arrival should coincide with the announcement of my departure.

The second providence concerned the church building. In 1991 we knew that major work needed to be carried out on the roof, which would involve substantial strengthening of the whole building. It was to be a very costly exercise, but I was humbled when I saw the selfless generosity of so many within the fellowship. Seeing their commitment to the church convinced me it could not be the Lord's will for me to then desert them. I had long felt that circumstances are a major factor in guidance and those providences of 1991 served as a confirmation.

In the pastoral and preaching ministry there are, of course, trials and disappointments, but the only real regrets I have are with myself. The Lord blessed the church and when I retired, the membership was in excess of fifty, but if I had been more prayerful, more faithful, more Christ-centred, then who knows what further blessings we might have received.

When I retired from the pastorate, I was faced with the question of where to worship in retirement. Except where circumstances dictate, this has been, and I suspect always will be, a dilemma for pastors. There are, perhaps, three options, each with accompanying advantages and disadvantages:

- remain in the same location and worship at the church where one has ministered;
- remain in the same location but worship at a different church;
- relocate to a new area and worship at a church in that area.

Pat and I rejected the first option, as we felt it might not be easy for a young pastor if the retired pastor was still in the congregation. Option three was not a consideration as, having a multi-handicapped son, it was not practical to move from our adapted accommodation. Therefore, we settled on option two, still living in Ingleton but worshipping eighteen miles away in Kendal. Not the ideal situation – and Pat, who does not drive, especially misses the day-to-day involvement she has always had with churches. The sacrifices which pastors' wives make as they support their husbands must never be underestimated, and this often continues into retirement.

It is easier for me, as I still have the preaching ministry and it is my prayer that whilst I have health, strength and the invitations to preach, this God-ordained activity will continue. Dr Martyn Lloyd-Jones said, "The work of preaching is the highest and the greatest and the most glorious calling to which anyone can be called." With this statement I fully concur, never ceasing to marvel that God should have entrusted the proclamation of His Word into the hands of weak and sinful men – even an 'earthen vessel' as weak and sinful as me.

Contact the Author

To contact the author, please write to:

John Mollitt,
Westgate,
Croft Road,
Ingleton,
Carnforth,
Lancs.
LA6 3BZ

Or send an email to:

john.mollitt@btinternet.com

Also by John Mollitt

Truth in a Nutshell
John Mollitt
ISBN 978-1-910197-76-9

Small bites of Bible wisdom for daily nourishment.

This book of meditations contains over 100 scriptures and anecdotes. Taken from the life and experiences of itinerant preacher, John Mollitt, each story illustrates a key lesson from the scripture being studied. Organised by topic, these short pieces are perfect both for daily readings and as a resource for Bible teaching.

Available from **www.onwardsandupwards.org** and all good bookshops.

Publisher's Recommendation

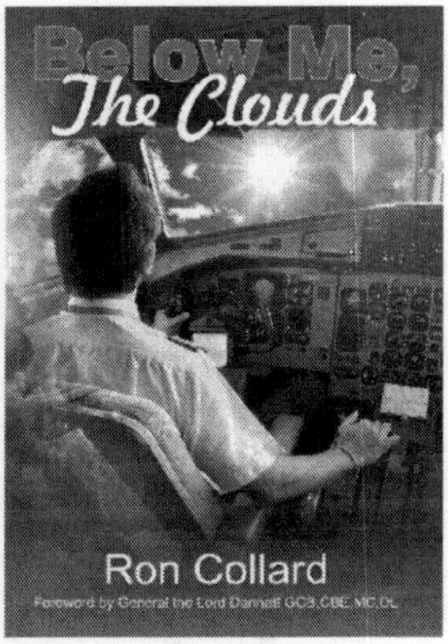

Below Me, The Clouds
Ron Collard
ISBN 978-1-907509-31-5

The life story of RAF and MAF pilot, Ron Collard.

"Climbing through solid cloud and breaking into a new world of sunshine and dazzling blue sky has been my delightful experience on numerous occasions. My life has been like that: living through clouds of war, fear, illness, disappointment, heart-ache, anxiety, failure and despair. I have, however, been lifted through them and above them – not by my own native wit, intelligence or wisdom but by a Power outside of my limited being, yet discernible in history and in the rough and tumble of modern everyday life. This book will encourage you to climb higher and view the 'clouds' of your life from a different perspective and, in so doing, to be introduced to the most wonderful Friend who can bring you 'out of darkness into His marvellous light'."

Available from **www.onwardsandupwards.org**
and all good bookshops.